GREAT RECI

TO PAIR WITH

SHITTY WINE

Craig Choisser

John Choisser

Copyright © 2018 Craig Choisser and John Choisser
All rights reserved.

No part of this publication may be reproduced, distributed, or transmitted in any form or by any means, including photocopying, recording, or other electronic or mechanical methods, without the prior written permission of the publisher, except in the case of brief quotations embodied in reviews and certain other non-commercial uses permitted by copyright law.

ISBN 978-1986241748

Printed in the United States of America

Published by Readerplace Books, LLC
www.readerplace.com

Special thanks to the Cooking Dude (aka John) for contributing many of the recipes contained herein. Many of these recipes and many, many more can be found at CookingDude.com, or in one of the many Cooking Dude cookbooks available at Amazon.

GREAT RECIPES

TO PAIR WITH

SHITTY WINE

Contents

Wine Shame.

We've all felt it. Not the kind that comes with the snooty sommelier looking over his nose at you. No, we mean the kind that comes from trying the "too good to be true" $6 bottle at Costco and finding out there's a perfectly good explanation for why that phrase exists. At the supermarket we look up at the top shelf with longing, then gradually down to the middle shelves, and, ultimately to the bottom shelves where there must, *must*, be a deal to be had. Sometimes it pays off.

There's no better feeling than finding The Great Wine Deal - often countered by the abject sadness one feels when, upon returning to the store to stock up, finding that the unwashed masses (the *other* unwashed masses) have caught on to it. But, as often as not, we end up with bottles of wine that even we peasants struggle to gag down. What now? Toss it? Pretend that we'll turn it into red wine vinegar (i.e. toss it later)? No, we beat it into submission, and figure out how to enjoy it anyway.

Usually you want balance between food and wine. We love a cab that can stand up to a hearty steak, or an acidic Chianti that dances with a tomato sauce like Fred and Ginger. Not here. Here you want the food to grab the wine in a bear hug, subdue it and make it behave. Like when your kid comes home from his freshman year at college.

Pairing with good wine is pretty easy, and there are a thousand references for you to check out. But when have you seen food suggestions to pair with something "rank" or "brackish?" "Disobedient" or "ghastly" or even "life threatening?"

Truly there is an art to paring good food with bad wine, and we have little doubt in our minds that we have come nowhere close to mastering it. Not for lack of trying, we assure you. We're not sommeliers, and we pick wines at restaurants the same way you do. What are we? We are cooking nerds, we love wine, and we're cheap. Seriously cheap.

But fear not, the recipes in this book are great, easy, and mostly fast, so while the novelty of the shitty wine pairing will surely wear off, we think the recipes will almost certainly find their way into your everyday repertoire. Buy a few copies of this book for friends, and maybe someday we can afford to buy a bottle that's not on the bottom shelf…not that we'd know what to eat with it.

General Tips for Drinking Bad Wine

1. Drink it colder than usual. Not just whites, but reds as well. Quality reds should be stored at about 55 degrees, and served somewhere in the low 60s. This is actually below room temperature. If you have a shitty red don't be afraid to serve it right out of the refrigerator. It will warm up quickly in the glass, and it helps dull some of the harsh edges, mute some of the aromas and depress the more off-putting flavor notes.

2. If you're chilling a white, put some water into an ice bucket, add ½ cup of table salt and stir. Then add the ice. The salt will lower the water temperature even further, allowing for an extra layer of flavor dulling.

3. Decant it and aerate the hell out of it. You can even put it in a blender. We'd feel bad for the blender, but there's no better way to get air in there.

4. Don't sip right away; give the food a chance to work on your mouth first. Foods that are higher in fat and salt seem to have the most pronounced effects.

5. Glutamates! This is where life as a cooking nerd pays off. Foods such as Parmesan cheese, tomato paste, soy sauce, mushrooms and Worcestershire sauce are high in glutamates, which is what gives us those glorious umami bombs. The recipes in this book have tried to incorporate glutamates wherever possible for precisely this reason.

Rank Reds

We're not going into too much detail with respect to each varietal. But, much like your first day in prison, find the toughest wine and show them who's boss. If you can beat down a bad cab, you can absolutely take out a horrible pinot. A bad pinot is the scrawny nerd of the bad wine world.

When it comes to reds we've discovered there are actually two different kinds of shitty – reds that are high in alcohol and tannins and thus really bitter, and those that have a sweet and heavy profile. (Tannins are the astringent components of wine that give it dryness but also that bitter, puckering sensation in your mouth.) The sweeter heavier reds are likely to be shitty wines that the winery just couldn't send out as is, and so they used various additives to soften the edges of the wine. The blending or additives can make brackish swill into something a little more palatable, but as often as not, they overshoot and it starts tasting like Manischewitz. Bleh.

The best way to handle an unruly red is with fat and salt; this works for either sweet or bitter high alcohol reds. For bitter reds BBQ can also a good way to go, but go with a sweet sauce to tamp down the tannins and alcohol - a North Carolina vinegar-based sauce can actually make things worse. If the wine tastes like the winemaker added grape juice to it in a transparent and futile effort to "soften the edges" sweet BBQ would not be a good way to go. Spice is your friend here. Try the Rooster Sauce or Chipotle Short Ribs. The goal here is to do what you would otherwise not do with a good red – mute it. And enjoy it, once expectations have been sufficiently lowered. Cheers!

Tri Tip and Pinto Bean Chili

Serves 6-8
Shitty Wine Beaters: Spice, Salt

Notes: Tri tip is an amazing cut of meat – it's one of very few cuts that work well braised, grilled or roasted. The tomato jalapeno sauce is nice shortcut, adding spice in a tomato base. It can be found in the international section of most grocery stores or online. After adding the flour, the mixture may look dry and clumpy. Don't panic. The flour helps thicken the chili, and the clumps will vanish once the liquid has been added. Just keep stirring and mashing the flour clumps to ensure that no raw uncooked flour taste ends up in the finished chili. The second "drop" of the chili powder allows for a fresher chili bite, rather than simply adding all at the beginning of cooking. You can taste the chili at the two hour mark and see if you want the additional spice. You can use a pressure cooker to speed things up a bit, up through step 11. Once the beans are added you don't want to put it back under pressure in case the beans all blow out. Cook under pressure for 45 minutes to 1 hour, with natural release. Add beans and simmer slowly until beef is tender and chili has thickened.

1	4 pound Tri Tip roast	5	cloves garlic, minced or pressed
2	onions, chopped	1	tablespoon flour
1	red bell pepper, chopped	1	4 ounce can El Pato tomato jalapeno sauce
1	tablespoon tomato paste		
1	tablespoon ground cumin	1	4 ounce can tomato sauce
1	tablespoon oregano	2	cups chicken stock
2	tablespoons chili powder, divided	3	15 ounce cans pinto beans, drained
1	teaspoon salt		

1. Preheat oven to 275 degrees.
2. Cut beef into 1/2 inch pieces.
3. Heat 2 tablespoons vegetable oil in large Dutch oven over high heat until almost smoking.
4. Brown beef in batches, about 1/3 of beef for each batch, for 6-8 minutes total per batch.
5. Lower heat to medium high. Add 1 tablespoon vegetable oil to now empty pot and add onion, bell pepper and tomato paste.
6. Cook, stirring frequently, until onion and peppers are soft and tomato paste has browned, about 6 minutes.
7. Add cumin, oregano, 1 tablespoon chili powder, and salt. Cook stirring constantly, allowing spices to bloom in oil, about 1 minute.
8. Add garlic and cook for 30 seconds.
9. Add flour and cook for 2 minutes, stirring constantly, to cook off raw flour taste.
10. Add tomato jalapeno sauce, tomato sauce, and chicken stock and stir vigorously to break up any flour clumps. Scrape up any browned bits from the bottom of the pot.
11. Bring to a boil, add beef back into Dutch oven and transfer to oven.
12. After 2 hours, remove Dutch oven from oven and add drained pinto beans and 1 tablespoon chili powder. Return to oven for up to 1 additional hour, or until meat is tender and sauce is flavorful.

Bacon Cheeseburger Meatloaf

Serves 8-10

Shitty Wine Beaters: Fat, Salt, Fat, Salt, repeat

Notes: This meatloaf starts with the Bacon in the Beef Burger mixture. When grinding the meat look for a texture that is not quite a fine as store bought ground beef, but still holds together. White American cheese can usually be found at the deli counter, have them cut a chunk for you to cube or grate rather than using individually wrapped singles. When you cube it the cheese melts, but stays in little pockets, which meet up in little fissures of molten cheese magma. Fantastic. Cooking on a rimmed baking sheet instead of loaf pan allows for more browning, and allows excess fat to drain away from the meatloaf. The best way to eat this meatloaf is the following day, or several hours after making it. Cut 1 inch slices off the loaf, then lay the slices cut side down in preheated nonstick skillet with 2 teaspoons vegetable oil. Putting a nice sear on the cut sides of the meatloaf makes for extra flavor, and the cheese in the meatloaf will melt a bit and contact the pan – and the toasty cheese takes this to the next level.

3	pounds flap meat	¼	cup milk
1	pound thick cut bacon	3	eggs
½ - ¾	pound white American cheese, in ¼ cubes, or coarsely grated	½	cup ketchup, plus glaze
		1	teaspoon Worcestershire sauce
1	medium onion finely diced or grated	1	teaspoon garlic powder
		2	teaspoons salt
2	cups panko bread crumbs	2	teaspoons pepper

1. Cut flap meat and bacon into 1 inch chunks, arrange on rimmed baking sheet with space between.
2. Put baking sheet into freezer for about 20-25 minutes, until meat is firm but not completely frozen.
3. Preheat oven to 375 degrees, with rack in middle position.
4. In a food processor fitted with chopping blade, process bacon/beef chunks in batches using short 1 second pulses, about 15-20 pulses total.
5. Transfer meat to a rimmed baking sheet, and repeat grinding with other batches of bacon/beef mixture.
6. Once all meat is ground and on baking sheet, quickly sort through meat looking for any large or stringy pieces of fat and discard.
7. In large mixing bowl, whisk the eggs, then add the panko and milk and mix. Add ground meat mixture and all other ingredients and gently mix thoroughly with your hands, trying to avoid overworking meat.
8. Put a tablespoon of the mixture on a microwave safe plate and microwave for 30 seconds or until no pink remains. Taste microwaved sample, and adjust seasonings as needed.
9. On foil lined rimmed baking sheet, shape meat mixture into rectangular loaf, about 3-4 inches high.
10. Brush loaf with thin layer of ketchup.
11. Bake until instant read thermometer reads 155 degrees. The meatloaf will continue cooking to 160 degrees while resting.
12. Slice and serve. If you want to sear slices in hot skillet, let meatloaf cool for at least 30 minutes to firm up before slicing.

Classic Meat Loaf

Serves 6-8
Shitty Wine Beaters: Fat, Salt

Notes: There are hundreds of lousy meat loaves made and served every day. We've made some of them, while experimenting with new ideas. Like adding oatmeal – which makes it gummy. Or low fat meat – which makes it dry and hard to swallow. This one is a guaranteed crowd pleaser, perfect with mashed potatoes on a cold day.

3	pounds hamburger, 85% lean	1	tablespoon prepared mustard, preferably Dijon style
1	pound breakfast sausage, either regular or hot	¼	cup ketchup
2	medium stalks of celery, chopped fine	1	tablespoon A1 sauce
1	medium onion, chopped fine	1	tablespoon Worcestershire sauce
2	eggs	½	teaspoon Tabasco
¼	cup milk	¼	cup dried parsley flakes
¼	cup breadcrumbs, preferably seasoned	2	teaspoons garlic salt
		1	teaspoon black pepper

1. Preheat oven to 375 degrees.
2. In a large bowl, break up the sausage and hamburger into pieces and let them come up to room temperature while prepping other ingredients.
3. In a medium bowl, break the two eggs, add the milk and stir.
4. Add the breadcrumbs, mustard, ketchup, A1 sauce, Worcestershire sauce, Tabasco, parsley flakes, garlic salt and pepper to egg mixture and stir to combine.
5. Add the chopped vegetables to egg mixture, and stir again.
6. Add egg/vegetable mixture to the large bowl containing meat.
7. Knead meat mixture gently with hands until well mixed, without overworking the meat.
8. Put a tablespoon of the mixture on a microwave safe plate and microwave for 30 seconds or until no pink remains. Taste microwaved sample, and adjust seasonings as needed.
9. On foil lined rimmed baking sheet, shape meat mixture into rectangular loaf, about 3-4 inches high.
10. Bake for about 45 minutes, until the tops are brown and the interior temperature reaches 140 degrees.
11. Remove from the oven and let cool for 15 minutes before slicing.

Dr. Pepper Ham

Serves 10-12

Shitty Wine Beaters: Sweet, Salt

Notes: You can use Coke or Pepsi or whatever your favorite is for this recipe, and either way, we bet you and your guests like it better than honey. Generally when you buy a spiral sliced ham, it will include a package containing the instant ingredients for a glaze, including honey buds. It's not bad, but don't feel bad about throwing away that packet and using this glaze. You can buy excellent pre-cut spiral sliced ham at Costco or other markets. The glaze can be made the day before or earlier if needed. The ham is already cooked, so all you really need to do is to warm it up. If you cook it too long, it will lose moisture and flavor. Some prefer their ham close to room temperature, others prefer it piping hot, just know that the hotter it gets the more moisture and flavor it loses. Perhaps not ideal for pairing with a crappy sweet red wine, but this ham is perfect for overly alcoholic and tannic reds and acidic whites.

½	cup Dr. Pepper
¾	cup light brown sugar
2	tablespoons orange juice
2	tablespoons Dijon mustard
1	spiral sliced bone-in half ham, 7-10 pounds

1. Unwrap the ham, remove the plastic bone cover, and place in baking dish flat side down. Wrap the ham with foil and let sit at room temperature for 1-2 hours.
2. Put oven rack at low position and preheat oven to 250 degrees.
3. Put baking dish with ham into oven and cook for about 1 hour to get warm, or about 2 hours to get to 120 degrees.
4. While ham is warming, put the Dr. Pepper, sugar, orange juice, and mustard in a sauce pan and bring to a simmer. The mustard is hard to dissolve, so use a whisk and stir constantly. Simmer the glaze for about 10 minutes, and remove from the heat.
5. Remove ham from oven, remove the foil, and paint the glaze on with a brush. Put it back in the oven for 10-15 minutes to set the glaze, and then remove the ham from the oven, paint it again with glaze, and cover until serving.
6. For beautiful serving slices, lay ham on its side and make three or four cuts into the ham along the fat line.

Chipotle Short Ribs

Serves 4-5
Shitty Wine Beaters: Fat, Salt, Spice

Notes: This recipe will serve four or five, so if you need to increase it, it's easy to do. Chipotle chiles are dried and smoked jalapeño chiles. They are easy to find in most supermarkets, usually packed in adobo sauce. This recipe uses enough to add a great depth of flavor without making the dish overly spicy. You can use a premade branded rub mix, but you can easily make your own. Rubs are almost always based on paprika or chili powder, or both, and include garlic salt, pepper, cumin, coriander and so forth. See below for a typical (but delicious) rub. This is very versatile recipe that goes just as well with mashed potatoes as it does with warm tortillas and Spanish rice. Just make sure you have something to soak up the sauce. To finish the dish, seed and slice 3 fresh California (Anaheim) chiles into ¼ inch rings, along with chopped cilantro and lime wedges.

2-3	pounds beef short ribs	1	cup drained diced tomatoes
2	tablespoons (or more, if needed) olive oil	1/4	cup fresh lime juice (about two limes)
2	cups onion, chopped	2	tablespoons chopped canned chipotle chiles
6	garlic cloves, minced		
2	cups beef broth		

BBQ Rub:

1 teaspoon each of garlic salt, black pepper, ground cumin, chili powder and ½ teaspoon coriander

1. Coat the ribs generously on all sides and put in zipper lock bag for at least an hour, or up to one day.
2. Preheat the oven to 350 degrees.
3. Heat the oil in a large oven-proof pot or Dutch oven, until smoking.
4. Brown the ribs a few at a time for 2-3 minutes on each side.
5. Remove ribs and set aside.
6. Reduce heat to medium and add the onion and garlic.
7. Cook, stirring frequently for 3-4 minutes.
8. Add the broth and bring to a boil, scraping the bottom of the pot to loosen the brown bits left over from the ribs.
9. Add the tomatoes, lime juice and chipotles and mix well. Add the ribs back into the pot rib side up, pushing them down into the liquid. Cover the pot, bring it to a boil, and put in the oven for 1 1/2 hours.
10. Remove the pot from the oven, place on the stove, and tilt it so you can spoon off some of the fat.
11. Simmer uncovered for 45 minutes to thicken the sauce. During the last 10 minutes, add the sliced Anaheim chile rings and season with salt and pepper.
12. Serve with potato, noodles, or tortillas, garnished with the chopped cilantro and lime wedges.

Bacon in the Beef Burgers

Serves 4
Shitty Wine Beaters: Fat, Salt, More Fat

Notes: Flap meat is sometimes referred to as steak tips. The partial freezing of the meat is a crucial step, if you skip it the fat in the meat and bacon will not get chopped but instead get stretched into long thin strands that end up stringy in the meat. Trust us, grinding your own meat is worth the extra steps. In Step 3, the meat should be coarsely ground, not as finely ground as traditional supermarket ground beef. Too fine a grind will make the meat too compact and dense. Because the burgers are better when loosely packed, it's difficult to salt and pepper both sides prior to cooking. Season the first side when burgers go into the pan, then the second side when the patties are flipped. Because these are loose patties, they will not work well on a grill and will likely break apart and fall into the fire. Then you have bad wine and no food. Be careful when seasoning with salt, the bacon in the burgers is salty and you don't want to over season. Put some butter or mayo on the bottom bun. The fat creates a barrier between bun and meat to help keep meat juices from making bun soggy.

1	pound flap meat
½	pound bacon
4	slices American cheese, if desired
4	hamburger buns
	burger toppings as desired

1. Cut flap meat and bacon into 1 inch chunks, arrange on rimmed baking sheet with space between.
2. Put baking sheet into freezer for about 20-25 minutes, until meat is firm but not completely frozen.
3. Preheat 12 inch cast iron skillet over high heat.
4. In a food processor fitted with chopping blade, process about 1/3 of bacon/beef chunks using short 1 second pulses, about 12-15 pulses total.
5. Transfer meat to a rimmed baking sheet, and repeat grinding with other batches of bacon/beef mixture.
6. Once all meat is ground and on baking sheet, quickly sort through meat looking for any large or stringy pieces of fat and discard.
7. Leaving meat on baking sheet, shape meat into four fairly loose 4 inch patties that hold their shape but are not tightly packed.
8. Using spatula transfer burgers from baking sheet to now hot skillet, set timer for 2 minutes, and season top of burgers with salt and pepper. You do not need to add any oil to skillet.
9. After 2 minutes, carefully flip burgers and season second side with salt and pepper. After 1 minute put cheese slices on burger (if desired) and cook 1 minute longer.
10. Put burgers on toasted buttered buns and top as desired.

Smash burger: Follow steps above through Step 6. Form meat into 3 ounce balls, but not tightly packed. Place 2 balls into hot skillet and immediately smash down into thin patties using wide BBQ spatula, use force to maximize skillet contact. Cook for about 1 minute, then scrape up the patties making sure to get crust off skillet bottom (metal bench scraper works well). Flip, add cheese, and cook for one more minute.

Cast Iron Skillet Pizza

Serves 4
Shitty Wine Beaters: Fat, Salt

Notes: Bad wine needs good pizza. Trader Joes makes a great pre-made pizza dough. Feel free to make your own, we'd rather spend the time drinking bad wine. A 12 inch cast iron skillet is the perfect size for the pre-made dough balls, if you have a 10 inch skillet cut off and discard about 20% of the dough or the pizza will be too thick. For a thinner crust use about 12 ounces of dough for 12 inch skillet, and 8 ounces for a 10 inch. Typically pizza recipes call for the hottest setting for an oven, but in this case an oven that is 500 degrees or more will start to burn the outside of the pizza before the inside has cooked. The result is doughy undercooked pizza. Toppings are, of course, a matter of personal choice, we happen to like the ones below. Just keep in mind this is a thick crust pizza.

1	Pre-made pizza dough		3	ounces pepperoni slices
¾	cup Basic Tomato Sauce (see page 84)		½	small onion sliced
1 ½	cups shredded mozzarella cheese		¼	cup sliced pepperoncini rings

1. Add 1 tablespoon olive oil to skillet and swirl to coat.
2. Put dough in skillet and let sit at room temperature for about an hour.
3. Preheat oven to 450 degrees.
4. Flip dough to coat all sides with oil, then push dough into the corners of skillet, covering the entire bottom of skillet.
5. Spread tomato sauce over dough, all the way to the edges.
6. Sprinkle cheese on top, and layer on onion, pepperoni, and other toppings.
7. Place skillet in oven and bake, about 15 minutes.
8. Check pizza crust for doneness by removing skillet and using spatula to peek underneath pizza.
9. Remove from skillet, slice and serve.

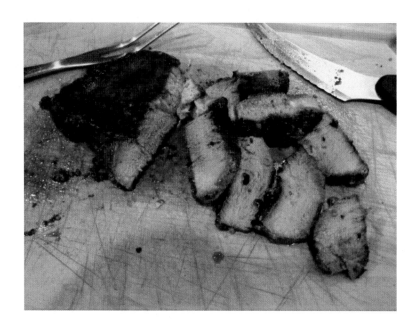

New York Steak Arrachera

Serves 4

Shitty Wine Beaters: Fat, Salt, Acid

Notes: Arrachera is a delicious Mexican steak made from skirt steak, but you can try any steak fixed this way. The New York cut is our favorite. Rib steaks are more flavorful, but they have more fat and gristle than New York or Filet Mignon. Filet Mignon is more tender, but doesn't have as much flavor. The New York is the best compromise. For three pounds of steak, this recipe makes enough marinade. You obviously can adjust the quantities up or down as you need. Setting aside some marinade before adding the steaks is an easy way to add a flavor kick at the end to the cooked steak. If you don't have much time, you can marinate the steaks for only 1/2 hour or so, but an hour or two is better. The marinade isn't very salty, so you will probably want to add some salt along with more pepper at serving. A side of beans and a simple salad will finish off the meal, maybe with some warm tortillas on the side, along with a glass of ruthless red wine.

3	lbs. steak, preferably New York strip

Marinade:

3	tablespoons chopped garlic
1/2	onion, sliced
3	tablespoons olive oil
3	tablespoons lime juice
1/4	teaspoon cumin
1	teaspoon salt
1	teaspoon pepper

1. Preheat gas or charcoal grill.
2. Combine all marinade ingredients
3. Reserve 1-2 tablespoons marinade in small bowl and set aside.
4. Place steaks in zipper lock bags, add marinade (except reserved portion) and marinate the steaks for a minimum of 1/2 hour, preferably 1 to 2 hours.
5. Dry steaks (to promote browning) and grill for 3-4 minutes per side for medium rare.
6. If you measure their temperature with an instant read thermometer (which is highly recommended), you should pull the steaks off at about 130 degrees.
7. Let steaks rest for 5 minutes (temperature will continue to rise to about 135).
8. Slice on the diagonal, dress with reserved marinade and serve.

Italian Wine Braised Beef

Serves 6
Shitty Wine Beaters: Fat, Salt, Acid

Notes: Bonus! One crappy bottle to drink, one to cook with! You need to use a cut of beef intended for braising like a chuck roast or boneless short ribs (which are actually cut from the chuck). Bone in short ribs will work but they are really fatty and the yield is lower so adjust accordingly. A very low oven is the best for keeping the meat tender and juicy. Speed it up at your peril. A tea ball (used for making tea with loose tea leaves) is an easy way to add herbs to stews and makes for easy retrieval before serving. Otherwise wrap herbs in cheesecloth and tie to secure. A fat separator with a built in strainer is ideal for defatting the braising liquid. This can also be made in a pressure cooker, although the sauce is not quite as complex. Follow the same steps below, but in a pressure cooker rather than Dutch oven. Cook for 45 minutes to an hour, and use natural release at the end to prevent boiling. Defat and reduce sauce as below. Serve with mashed potatoes or over egg noodles.

1	4 lb chuck roast or boneless short ribs, cut in 2 inch cubes	1	14 ounce can diced tomatoes, drained
2	onions	1	bottle shitty red wine
	kosher salt	2	sprigs fresh rosemary
	black pepper	2	springs fresh thyme
3	cloves garlic	5	sprigs fresh parsley
1	tablespoon tomato paste	1	bay leaf
1	tablespoon flour		

1. Heat oven to 275 degrees and put rack at lower middle position.
2. Cube beef into 2 inch cubes, and remove any hard or large pieces of fat. Do not trim excessively.
3. In large (6-8qt) dutch oven, heat 1 tablespoon vegetable oil over high heat (use bacon fat or duck fat, if available).
4. Salt and pepper beef cubes, and add half of cubes to pot. Brown thoroughly on all sides in two batches (to avoid crowding meat), about 6-8 minutes for each batch. Add additional fat and adjust heat as needed. Allow (encourage!) fond to develop in bottom of pot, but if fond looks too dark, add 1 tablespoon water (to deglaze) before it begins to burn (but do not clean out pot, we want to keep the flavor in there). Remove beef and set aside in clean dish.
5. Heat 1 tablespoon oil in now empty pot, and add onion and tomato paste. Lower heat to medium and cook stirring occasionally until onion is soft and tomato paste starts to brown. Allow fond to develop in bottom of pot, but if fond looks too dark, add 1 tablespoon water (to deglaze) before it begins to burn.
6. Add garlic and cook for 30 seconds until fragrant.
7. Lower heat to medium low, add flour to onion mixture and cook, stirring constantly, for 2-3 minutes until all flour has been incorporated and raw flour smell has been cooked off. Mixture will appear very dry and clumpy, continue to break it up and stir it. It's important to ensure that there is no raw flour taste in the final dish.

8. Add about half the bottle of wine, increase heat to high, and whisk vigorously to break up flour and onion mixture. Once all lumps are whisked away, add reminder of wine and drained diced tomatoes.
9. Add beef to pot and poke to submerge.
10. Add parsley and bay leaf to pot. Put rosemary and thyme into cheesecloth or loose tea ball and add to pot.
11. Cover Dutch oven with lid until simmering vigorously, then put into oven for 3 hours, covered, stirring halfway. Check beef for doneness after 3 hours, paring knife should slide in easily.
12. Remove Dutch oven from oven, remove herbs and discard. Remove beef and transfer into clean dish and cover to keep warm.
13. Defat the braising liquid. The best way is to strain the vegetables from the liquid (but do no throw them out) and pour the liquid into a fat separator, wait 5 minutes and pour defatted liquid (and vegetable pieces) back into pot. Or wait 5 minutes and use a wide spoon to skim fat from surface.
14. Once defatted braising liquid and vegetables have been transferred back into Dutch oven, use immersion blender to break down vegetables. Heat braising liquid to boil and cooked until reduced, thickened and flavorful, about 10 minutes. Adjust heat to low, add beef back to pot to warm through. Adjust seasonings as needed.

Crappy Whites

One word. Cold.

The best part about whites is that they are already served cold, and this is clearly the best way to neutralize abrasive white wines. Take it to the next level and add salt to a bucket of ice water to take it down to the edge of freezing. A winesicle is probably not a bad way to go, but makes for poor table manners.

As with Crappy Reds, salt and spice help dull your ability to taste bitter flavors so those are always helpful. Use spice if your Chardonnay tastes like Skittles, perhaps the Jerk Chicken or Shrimp Fra Diavola. Speaking of Chardonnay …it's often so heavily and artificially oaked it feels like you're getting splinters in your tongue. Evidently there is a process that takes what are essentially giant tea bags of burnt wood chips and dunks them into cheaply made Chardonnay to add smoke flavors. Yes, your wine may have been tea bagged. Counter that with burgers – and bacon! As if we need an excuse to eat more bacon.

In the case of an acidic shitty white wine you'll want to ensure that the acid in the food is dominant. The tomatoes in our Tilapia Sorrento or the vinegar in Grandma's Green beans or German Red Cabbage are just what the doctor ordered. Another option is the strong flavors and mouth-coating effects of butter and cream, so good old fashioned Mashed Potatoes or the Bacon Leek Swiss quiche will help take the edge off. Cheers!

Jerk Chicken

Serves 4
Shitty Wine Beaters: Spice, Salt

Notes: It helps here if you have a food processor to make the jerk paste for marinating the chicken, but if you don't, just mince the ingredients the best you can. It's more work, but the flavor will be the same. This chicken is intended to be cooked outside on the grill, but works equally well it in the oven. So if you prefer, grill it outside and ignore the instructions below for the oven. As is always the case for chicken, don't have the grill too hot (medium heat) because you don't want the sauce to burn. Cook it gently for about 45 minutes, turning it every 10 minutes or so.

1	3-4 pound chicken, cut up	¼	cup lime juice (approximately one lime)
½	yellow or brown onion, or 1 bunch of green onions (about eight)	¼	cup vegetable oil
1	tablespoon powdered ginger	1	tablespoon black pepper
4	cloves garlic	1	tablespoon salt
3	jalapeño chiles	2	teaspoons ground allspice
3	bay leaves	1	teaspoon ground nutmeg
2	tablespoons fresh thyme, or 1 tablespoon dried	1	teaspoon ground cinnamon

1. Add ¼ cup kosher salt to 1 quart water in 3 quart container. Mix thoroughly and submerge chicken in brine for 30-60 minutes.
2. While it's brining, make the jerk paste.
3. In food processor, cut the onion into one inch chunks, crumble up the bay leaves, cut off the stem from the chiles and quarter them, and place all the ingredients in the food processor. Pulse it until you have a paste, about 10 pulses.
4. Preheat oven to 375 F.
5. Remove chicken from brine and pat dry. Put them in zipper lock bag with the jerk paste and let them marinate for 30-60 minutes.
6. Spread aluminum foil over a rimmed baking sheet and spray with cooking spray. Place the chicken pieces with the larger pieces on the outside, and roast for 45 minutes or until breast is 160 degrees and dark meat is 175 degrees.

Chicken Loco

Serves 6-8
Shitty Wine Beaters: Spice, Salt

Notes: This grilled chicken recipe came about in an effort to come close to the flavor of El Pollo Loco's grilled chicken. It's citrus-based, like theirs, but not quite the same. Annato (achiote) is a spice that not only provides flavor but also color. You need to grind up the seeds, and since they are pretty hard a spice grinder is handy here. If you can't find it, you can omit.

2	chickens, quartered	1	tablespoon cumin
6	ounces pineapple juice	1	tablespoon garlic powder
5	ounces orange juice	1	tablespoon chili powder
2	tablespoons lime juice	1	teaspoon oregano
2	tablespoons oil	1	teaspoon poultry seasoning
6	tablespoons apple cider vinegar	1	teaspoon salt
1	teaspoon black pepper	1	teaspoon ground annato (achiote)
1	teaspoon white pepper		

1. Quarter the chickens, rinse them off, and set them aside.
2. For the marinade mix all the other ingredients together, then set aside ¼ cup marinade for basting.
3. Pour remaining marinade into one or more plastic bags and add the chicken. Massage a little, and let marinate for at least 1/2 hour or up to a day refrigerated.
4. Heat gas grill or start charcoal grill (preferred) until hot.
5. Remove the chicken from the marinade. Grill the chicken over medium coals (or gas flame) for 40 -45 minutes, until the legs move freely, juice from the thigh runs clear, or the internal temperature gets up to 160 degrees for breast and 175 degrees F for dark meat. Turn the chicken every ten minutes or so during this period, and also move the pieces around so they cook as uniformly as possible. Once chicken is no longer raw on exterior (to prevent cross contamination), baste the chicken with the reserved marinade for the first 30 minutes.
6. A few flare-ups are OK, and adds flavor to the meat. If the flare-ups come up past the chicken and it's obviously going to turn the chicken to charcoal, move the chicken to a cooler part of the grill, and use a spray bottle to water down the flames if needed.
7. Serve with pinto beans and warmed corn tortillas.

Velveted Chicken Stir Fry

Serves 4-6
Shitty Wine Beaters: Spice, Salt

Notes: If you haven't tried velveting your chicken before this will come as a revelation. Usually stir fry pieces of chicken breast go from undercooked, to perfect, to overcooked literally in a matter of seconds. Brining helps, but velveting adds another layer of insurance, ensuring moist tender chicken even when cut into small stir fry size pieces. Low sodium soy sauce is a good idea here - since the sauce reduces regular soy sauce can become too salty. Lemongrass and ginger can often be found in toothpaste-like tubes in the fruit and vegetable section of the grocery store. They are easy to use and freeze well for months at a time. Stir frying in a cast iron skillet enables maximum heat, and even allows for some fond to develop in the bottom of the pan, which can be scraped up for added flavor when the sauce ingredients are added.

Chicken

2-3 large boneless skinless chicken breasts

2 tablespoons low sodium soy sauce

2 tablespoons water

1 tablespoon flour

1 tablespoon cornstarch

1 tablespoon sesame oil

1 tablespoon vegetable oil

Vegetables

2 cups broccoli florets

1 cup cauliflower florets

1 small onion, chopped

1 bell pepper

1 large carrot

1 zuchini or other squash

other veggies as desired

Sauce

¼ cup low sodium soy sauce

1 tablespoon sherry

2 teaspoons garlic chili paste

2 tablespoons water

1 tablespoon ginger and/or lemongrass

1 teaspoon cornstarch

1. Stir sauce ingredients together and set aside.
2. Cut chicken breast into 1 inch pieces.
3. Combine soy sauce and water and marinate chicken for 30 minutes.
4. While chicken marinates, chop all vegetables. Ensure that firmer vegetables (carrot, cauliflower, etc.) are roughly even in size.
5. Group vegetables by estimated cooking time: broccoli, cauliflower and carrot together. Onion, bell pepper and zucchini together, etc. You'll need to work in

whatever batch size required by your size skillet and amount of vegetables you are using.

6. Drain chicken from marinade and pat dry.

7. In a medium bowl combine flour, cornstarch, sesame oil and vegetable oil and mix into paste. Add chicken and stir to evenly coast chicken. Set aside.

8. Heat oil in 12 inch cast iron skillet until smoking. Add broccoli and/or cauliflower without overfilling pan, and cook for 2-3 minutes.

9. For longer cooking vegetables like broccoli and cauliflower, add 2 tablespoons water to skillet and cover to steam vegetables.

10. Remove lid and let water evaporate, continue cooking while stirring. Check to ensure vegetables are at desired doneness before transferring to clean bowl.

11. Repeat cooking process with each subsequent batch of vegetables, skipping steaming step for quicker cooking vegetables like onion and bell pepper, and adding vegetable oil as needed.

12. Once all vegetables are cooked, heat 1 tablespoon vegetable oil until hot and add half of chicken. Spread into even layer and cook without stirring for 2-3 minutes.

13. Stir chicken, and allow to brown on all sides, but check chicken after 5 minutes total cooking to ensure it does not overcook. Remove to clean bowl.

14. Repeat with second batch of chicken, remove to clean bowl.

15. Lower heat to medium, stir sauce mixture to recombine and add to skillet, scraping up browned bits from bottom of skillet. Sauce will thicken slightly, then quickly add vegetables and chicken back into skillet. Stir to combine and serve over steamed rice.

Shrimp Fra Diavolo

Serves 4
Shitty Wine Beaters: Spice, Salt

Notes: "Fra Diavolo" means "Brother Devil", and is a classic Italian dish. It's spicy, so it's not for wimps. This is a variation on the excellent recipe from Cooks Illustrated. Getting the ingredients ready before you start to cook is especially important here. You don't want the shrimp to cook to ashes while you rummage through your liquor cabinet looking for that bottle of cognac you've put somewhere. This dish goes fast, you won't have time to mince the garlic after you start cooking.

1	pound large shrimp (31 to 40 per pound)	½	teaspoon sugar
1	teaspoon red pepper flakes	1	28 ounce can diced tomatoes, drained
6	tablespoons olive oil	1	cup dry white wine
1	teaspoon salt	¼	cup minced fresh parsley leaves
¼	cup cognac or brandy	1	pound linguine or spaghetti
12	medium garlic cloves		

1. Put four quarts of water in a large pot, add 2 tablespoons salt, and drizzle in some olive oil, and bring to a boil. By the time you get the shrimp ready, it'll be ready to cook the pasta.
2. Mix the shrimp, half of the red pepper flakes, two tablespoons of the olive oil, and the salt in a bowl. Toss gently to evenly coat the shrimp.
3. Heat nonstick skillet over medium high heat. When hot, add the shrimp in a single layer and cook without stirring until they turn pink and get brown spots on the bottom. This only takes about a minute or so, depending on the heat of the skillet.
4. Take it off the heat, stir the shrimp, and add the cognac. Give it a few seconds to warm the cognac, and then wave a match or barbeque lighter over the skillet to ignite the cognac. Shake the pan a little to make sure it all gets a chance to burn off.
5. After the fire goes out, put the shrimp back in their bowl temporarily. Heat three tablespoons of the olive oil in the skillet over medium low heat, add 2/3 of the garlic, and cook, stirring constantly, for five or six minutes, until the garlic gets light brown. Don't let it burn, lower the heat or remove skillet from heat if needed. Add the other 1/2 teaspoon of the red pepper flakes, the salt, sugar, tomatoes, and wine. Simmer this sauce for ten minutes or so.
6. While sauce simmers, add pasta to boiling water, cook according to package directions, usually 9-12 minutes. Stir occasionally to keep the strands separated.
7. When the pasta seems soft, take out a strand, let it cool a little, and taste it. You'll know when it's too raw and when it feels "al dente", or chews properly. Reserve half a cup of the water with a coffee mug while it's cooking; for use in thinning the sauce later.

8. When the pasta is done, drain it well, and add the 1/2 cup of pasta water you saved earlier. Also add a few tablespoons of the sauce, and toss to coat the pasta. Now let the pasta sit covered to keep warm while you finish the dish in the skillet.
9. Put the shrimp, the rest of the garlic, and the parsley into the skillet with the sauce, spread it out gently, and cover it to re-warm the shrimp, 3-4 minutes.
10. Add shrimp to pasta, stir to combine and serve.

Chicken Parmesan

Serves 4
Shitty Wine Beaters: Salt, acid

Notes: Rather than soaking crispy chicken in tomato sauce until it gets soggy, this version allows the eater to add as much or as little sauce to their chicken at the end. The chicken stays crisp, cheese stays on the chicken and sauce provides a lighter and fresher finish. The frozen tenderloins will quickly bring the water up to room temperature to allow for safe defrosting. Table salt, Morton's kosher salt and other kosher salts vary in salinity. If using table salt cut amount by half. If using Diamond Crystal or other kosher salts use 25% additional salt. You can use a quality Parmesan, but the cheap grated stuff in the green can works well here and is substantially easier. Additional herbs or spices such as oregano or ground coriander can be added to breading mixture as desired.

8	chicken tenderloins	1	teaspoon ground pepper, white or black
½	cup Morton's kosher salt		olive oil
2	eggs		
2	tablespoons flour	8	ounces mozzarella, provolone or similar cheese, shredded
1 ½	cups panko		
½	cup Parmesan cheese	2	cups basic tomato sauce (see recipe page 84)
1	teaspoon kosher salt		flat leaf parsley, minced
1	teaspoon garlic powder		

1. If tenderloins are frozen, fill large container with 2 quarts hot water and stir in salt to dissolve. Add tenderloins and brine for at least 30 minutes, up to 90 minutes. If tenderloins are defrosted, use room temperature water.
2. Heat oven to "warm" setting or 180 degrees.
3. Add eggs to pie plate and whisk thoroughly. Add flour to plate and mix completely to combine.
4. In second pie plate mix together panko bread crumbs, Parmesan cheese, salt, white or black pepper and garlic powder.
5. Drain tenderloins and pat dry. Working with one tenderloin at a time, dredge in egg and flour mixture until coated, then let excess drip off. Lay tenderloin in panko mixture and coat thoroughly, pressing on mixture to adhere.
6. Place coated tenderloin on wire rack set in baking sheet. Repeat with all tenderloins.
7. Heat oil in large cast iron skillet until shimmering.
8. Add tenderloins without crowding (about 4 per batch) to skillet and cook about 1 minute and 45 seconds per side. Adjust heat as necessary to achieve proper browning.
9. Put cooked tenderloins on clean wire rack set in clean baking sheet and keep warm in oven.
10. When frying is complete, removed warmed tenderloins from oven and turn broiler to high. Place tenderloins in rimmed baking sheet and sprinkle with cheese.
11. Place baking sheet under broiler for approximately 3 minutes, until cheese is bubbling and slightly browned.
12. Plate tenderloins, saucing each portion individually with tomato sauce and sprinkling with chopped parsley.

Panko Chicken with Chile Sauces

Serves 4
Shitty Wine Beaters: Salt, spice

Notes: As in previous recipe, the frozen tenderloins will quickly bring the water up to room temperature to allow for safe defrosting. Table salt, Morton's kosher salt and other kosher salts vary in salinity. If using table salt, cut the amount used by half. If using Diamond Crystal or other kosher salts use 25% additional salt. You can use a quality Parmesan, but the cheap grated stuff in the green can works well here and is substantially easier. Additional herbs or spices such as oregano or ground coriander can be added to breading mixture as desired. Other dipping sauces can be used or created but, if you have a bad wine, ketchup (sweet) may not be a good way to go. Stick with spice and fat. Aji Amarillo paste is a South American chile paste and can be found online including Amazon. It's really good, and worth the effort to find.

8	chicken tenderloins	1	teaspoon garlic powder
½	cup Morton's kosher salt	1	teaspoon ground pepper, white or black
2	eggs		
2	tablespoons flour		olive oil
1 ½	cups panko	½	cup mayonnaise, divided
½	cup Parmesan cheese	1	tablespoon Sriracha
1	teaspoon kosher salt	1	tablespoon Aji Amarillo paste

1. If tenderloins are frozen, fill large container with 2 quarts hot water and stir in salt to dissolve. Add tenderloins and brine for at least 30 minutes, up to 90 minutes. If tenderloins are defrosted, use room temperature water.
2. Heat oven to "warm" setting or 180 degrees.
3. Add eggs to pie plate and whisk thoroughly. Add flour to plate and mix completely to combine.
4. In second pie plate mix together panko bread crumbs, Parmesan cheese, salt, white or black pepper and garlic powder.
5. Drain tenderloins and pat dry.
6. Working with one tenderloin at a time, dredge in egg and flour mixture until coated, let excess drip off. Lay tenderloin in panko mixture and coat thoroughly, pressing on mixture to adhere.
7. Place coated tenderloin on wire rack set in baking sheet. Repeat with all tenderloins.
8. Heat ¼ inch of oil in large cast iron skillet until shimmering.
9. Add tenderloins without crowding (about 4 per batch) to skillet and cook about 1 minute and 45 seconds per side. Adjust heat as necessary to achieve proper browning.
10. Put cooked tenderloins on clean wire rack set in clean baking sheet and keep warm in oven.
11. Add additional oil to skillet as needed.
12. Mix ¼ cup mayo with 1-2 tablespoons Sriracha and set aside.
13. Mix ¼ cup mayo with 1-2 tablespoons Aji Amarillo paste and set aside.
14. Serve tenderloins, passing sauces as desired.

Shrimp New Orleans

Serves 4

Shitty Wine Beaters: Acid, Salt

Notes: Here's a good shrimp recipe that cooks up in a jiffy and makes a simple but special dinner. For this recipe, try to find large shrimp, raw, shelled and deveined, with tails on. This recipe uses one pound of shrimp, which is enough for two dinners or four appetizers. Scale it up if necessary. Since this dish cooks quickly, make sure you prep side dishes, rice, etc. to go with the shrimp, if this is dinner instead of an appetizer.

1	pound shrimp, peeled, deveined, with tails left on	1	lemon, juiced and zest
10	garlic cloves, minced	8	sprigs fresh thyme
2	medium shallots or 2 tablespoons minced onion	2	tablespoons Worcestershire sauce
3	tablespoons black pepper	2	tablespoons hot sauce
1	tablespoon salt	½	bottle dark beer
		4	tablespoons butter

1. Combine everything except the butter in a bowl, mix, cover, and put it in the fridge for 1 to 6 hours.
2. Heat up a 12 inch nonstick skillet and add 2 tablespoons of the butter. Add the shrimp mixture and saute for about four minutes, until the shrimp are pink.
3. Remove the shrimp from the pan, leaving liquid behind in the skillet. Whisk in the remaining two tablespoons of the butter to make a sauce. Put the shrimp over rice, if using, and spoon the sauce over the shrimp. Use thyme sprigs as a garnish, or add paprika or other colorful garnish if desired.
4. Serve with French bread, olive oil, and a terrible white wine.

Shrimp Vera Cruz

Serves 4
Shitty Wine Beaters: Spice, Salt

Notes: This recipe is quick, easy and delicious. And it was smuggled out of a restaurant by a friendly waitress, and espionage always adds an air of intrigue to shrimp recipes. Use medium to large shrimp, and to save time and trouble, you can usually buy them peeled, de-veined, and frozen. One bag of 15-20 shrimp is enough for four servings. Serve it over rice, as shown, or in individual casserole dishes, or even in scallop shells if you have them. The sauce is delicious, so you'll want either rice, tortillas, or bread to soak up the excess.

12-15	medium or large shrimp, peeled and de-veined (shells left on tail for a handle)		cilantro, divided*
		1	cup shitty white wine
		8	tablespoons (one stick) butter, cut into several pieces
1	medium tomato, diced, divided*		
2	chopped green onions, or ¼ cup diced regular onion, divided*	2	teaspoons lemon juice
		1/2	teaspoon salt
4	tablespoons chopped fresh	1	teaspoon Tabasco

* These ingredients are used 1/2 for the sauce and 1/2 later for garnish.

1. In 12 inch skillet bring ½ of the tomato, ½ of the onion, ½ of the cilantro, the wine, lemon juice, salt and Tabasco to a simmer, cook for 5 minutes.
2. Add the shrimp and continue to simmer until the shrimp is pink, turning the shrimp once in a while. This will only take another five minutes or less. Remove the shrimp temporarily to a bowl, and whisk the butter into the sauce one piece at a time to make the sauce. After that's done, dump the shrimp back into the pan, turn off the heat and cover to keep warm.
3. Serve this with bad white wine and warm tortillas, garnish with remaining tomato, cilantro and onion.

Tilapia Sorrento

Serves 4

Shitty Wine Beaters: Acid, Salt

Notes: This is an absolutely delicious Italian recipe for baking or pan frying fish. You don't have to use tilapia; that just happens to be one of our favorites, but you can use flounder, halibut, catfish, or any reasonably mild fish.

4	Fish fillets or steaks	½	cup white wine
1	medium onion, chopped	¼	cup grated Parmesan cheese
1-2	plum or medium tomatoes per person, chopped		salt and pepper
		3	tablespoons olive oil
2	tablespoons capers, chopped	1	teaspoon oregano
8-12	pitted Kalamata olives, sliced	3	garlic cloves, minced

1. Heat the olive oil in a large nonstick skillet. Add the onion, and cook 3-4 minutes until soft. Add the garlic and cook one more minute. Then add the tomatoes, olives, capers, and oregano. Stir and simmer for five minutes.
2. Spoon vegetables out of the pan temporarily. Drizzle a little more olive oil in the pan, sprinkle the fish with salt and pepper, and lay them in the pan.
3. Sauté the fish for three or four minutes per side, depending on their thickness. Thin filets may cook even faster. Look at the edge of the fish; when the edge starts turning opaque, peek underneath to see if it's getting brown. Undercooking at this stage is better than overcooking, the fish will finish cooking after the next phase.
4. Remove the fish from the skillet to a plate, and return the vegetables to the skillet. Add the wine and scrape up the fond on the bottom of the pan. Stir the wine into the vegetables, simmer for 1 minute, then lay the fish on top. Cover the skillet for a few minutes to warm everything up.
5. Serve with grated Parmesan.

Bacon Leek Swiss Quiche

Serves 4
Shitty Wine Beaters: Fat, Salt

Notes: Classic Quiche Lorraine is an Egg McMuffin in a different format. This version features leeks for a subtle oniony-ness and swiss cheese. Look for leeks with a large white section, this recipe (like most) uses only the white and light green sections of the leek. Even if you like your bacon more tender than crisp, in this recipe it's best to cook the bacon until very crisp. Soft bacon cooked in the custard mix will get soggy and unpleasant, very crisp bacon can stand up to the moist cooking environment. Some people like to blind bake their tart shells for crisper crust, but it's always seemed like a hassle. Mixing the egg and evaporated milk mixture in a Pyrex 4 cup measuring cup makes it easy to pour into the party shell. Pressing pastry into pan carefully is key, the pastry will shrink during cooking, and if there's a gap it will shrink down the sides. Serve topped with avocado slices, pico de gallo or hot sauce, if desired.

2	leeks	1	can evaporated milk (not sweetened condensed)
½	pound bacon		
1	cup Swiss cheese, grated	2	eggs
1	frozen puff pastry sheet, square		salt and pepper

1. Defrost puff pastry in refrigerator overnight, or on counter for 2 hours. If it defrosts before you need to use it, put it in refrigerator until ready to use.
2. Preheat oven to 375 degrees, with rack in middle position.
3. Chop bacon in small ¼ inch pieces, then sauté in 10 inch nonstick skillet until very crisp. Remove with slotted spoon and drain on paper towels, leaving 1 tablespoon bacon fat in the skillet.
4. Cut stem ends and dark green ends off leeks, keeping white part and light green only. Slice in half length-wise and run under tap water to rinse out any dirt or sand, separating leaves with your fingers to rinse thoroughly.
5. Slice leeks into 1/8 inch half circles.
6. Heat skillet with reserved bacon fat to medium, then add leeks and ½ teaspoon salt.
7. Saute leeks slowly, without browning, until soft, about 10-12 minutes. Allow to cool.
8. In 4 cup measuring cup, whisk eggs until thoroughly blended. Add evaporated milk and stir to combine. Add 1 teaspoon freshly ground black pepper. Set aside.
9. Lightly dust large cutting board or counter with flour. Unfold defrosted puff pastry and push together any cracks with your fingers. Roll out puff pastry until it's about 25% larger than initial size and an even thickness.
10. Transfer puff pastry to 9-10 inch tart pan (removable bottoms are useful). No need to spray or butter it, the puff pastry has plenty of butter in it.
11. Work around the circumference of the pasty, press pastry down into bottom of pan and making sure there are no gaps between bottom and sides of pan. The pastry will shrink during cooking, and if there's a gap it will shrink down the sides.
12. Spread cooled leeks into bottom of pastry shell, you may not need to use them all. Add the bacon pieces. You'll definitely want to use them all. Add about ¾ of the cheese and spread around evenly. Add more as desired, depending on taste and size of tart pan.

13. To lower the chance of spilling, pull out oven rack and place tart pan directly on oven rack before adding egg mixture. If your oven rack sags, lift up on it slightly to level it, then pour egg mixture into tart pan until it reaches 1/4 inch below the top of the pan. You may have some mixture left over. You can also add additional cheese at this point if desired. If you have a removable bottom pan and are concerned about leaks, place a sheet pan on the rack directly below the tart. Slide rack into oven, and bake for 35-45 minutes, checking after 30 minutes.

14. Remove from oven and cool 5 minutes before serving.

Appetizers, Soups and Sides

We must admit, sometimes the appetizers, soups and sides are more of an afterthought than they should be. After brining and marinating and mincing and sautéing, who has time to think about the "extras" that go along with a meal? The kids think it's normal to pair braised chicken thighs with a banana. But when it comes to shitty wine, these forgotten heroes are your allies.

One of the key findings from drinking more bad wine than is advisable is that eating first helps get the mouth ready for the impending assault. So appetizers that feature fat, salt, spice and acid prepare your taste buds by hindering their ability to work on the wine.

When it comes to soups and sides, one of the apparently not-well-known rules of wine pairing is to pair with the dominant flavor on the plate. We picked some of our favorite side dishes with an eye towards working with your taste buds in the herculean effort to overcome the forces of evil wine.
Cheers!

Grilled Asparagus and Prosciutto

Serves 4-6

Shitty Wine Beaters: Salt, Fat

Notes: It's better to take too much off the bottom of the asparagus than it is to leave a woody, inedible portion in place. You can use a grill pan in the house, or even a cast iron skillet if necessary, but it's hard to get the same yield. You might have to work in batches. A decent Parmesan is key here, something that's aged a bit and is dry. Young, moist Parmesans are OK in a pinch, but the pre-grated stuff doesn't work.

1	bunch asparagus
1-2	3 oz. packages sliced prosciutto
4	tablespoon olive oil
2	tablespoons balsamic vinegar
1	teaspoon sugar
½	cup shaved good quality Parmesan cheese
	salt and pepper

1. Wash the asparagus and snap off the woody bottoms by hand. They should bend easily at the correct breaking point.
2. Put asparagus into large zipper lock bag, and add 2 tablespoons of the oil, 1 tablespoon balsamic vinegar, ½ teaspoon salt and ground black pepper. Close bag, and turn to coat asparagus, taking care not to break tips off.
3. Marinate for at least 30 minutes. Preheat grill to high.
4. In a small bowl combine 2 tablespoons olive oil, 1 tablespoon balsamic vinegar, sugar, and ½ teaspoon each of salt and pepper to make a vinaigrette. Mix thoroughly, taste to adjust seasoning, and set aside.
5. Use vegetable peeler to shave strips of Parmesan into a small clean dish. Set aside.
6. Remove asparagus from marinade and grill over hot grill until tender and a little charred in spots, turning frequently, about 5 minutes total (depending on how thick the asparagus are). Remove to platter.
7. Take one slice prosciutto and two spears of asparagus and wrap asparagus in prosciutto, starting at the bottom, and leaving asparagus tips exposed. Repeat with remaining asparagus and prosciutto.
8. Whisk vinaigrette to recombine and drizzle over asparagus. Sprinkle shaved Parmesan over asparagus and serve.

Endive and Blue Cheese Appetizer

Serves 6-8 as appetizer
Shitty Wine Beaters: Fat, Salt

Notes: The bitterness of the endive complements the strong blue cheese and sweetness of the apple. The "boat like" shape of the leaves make these appetizers easy to fill and eat.

2   heads Belgian endive
1   crisp apple, Gala, Cameo or similar
4   ounces blue cheese, crumbled
2   teaspoons fresh cracked black pepper, or to taste

1. Trim ¼ inch off stem ends of endive and separate leaves, repeating trimming and separating leaves until broken down into individual leaves. Arrange on platter.
2. Divide blue cheese between all endive leave, about 1-2 teaspoons per leaf.
3. Cut apple into quarters, then ¼ inch slices. Cut slices into matchsticks, then cut matchsticks into ¼ inch dice. Divide diced apple equally among all the endive leaves, about 1-2 teaspoons per leaf. Add coarsely ground black pepper to taste.

Cilantro Pesto

Cilantro Pesto

Shitty Wine Beaters: Acid, Salt

Notes: So it turns out pesto just means "paste." A bit of a revelation that opened up all kinds of pestos, including arugula and cilantro. This goes great with crudité like sliced bell pepper, or other dippers like toasted naan bread. You can use the stems, just trim off the bottom ¼ inch or so. If you want to take the bite out of the garlic, put the cloves in a mug with water and microwave for about 45 seconds prior to blending. Toast the pine nuts in a small dry skillet, swirling constantly until they smell toasty and nutty.

1	bunch cilantro	1/3	cup pine nuts, toasted
1	lime, zested and juiced	2	cloves garlic
2	tablespoons fresh oregano		salt and pepper
1/3	cup olive oil		

1. Blend all ingredients in a food processor or blender. Season to taste.

Red Onion Tomato Salad

Serves 4
Shitty Wine Beaters: Acid, Salt

Notes: Along with the Potatoes Lyonnaise, this simple salad is a version of one of our favorites at Morton's. But this one is a lot cheaper! Most supermarket tomatoes are not very good, farmer's market or heirloom tomatoes are better options. Most red onions have a very strong flavor, the pre-soak is an essential step.

2	large, in-season tomatoes, such as beefsteak
1	large red onion
4	cups cold water
2	tablespoons distilled white vinegar
½	cup blue cheese, crumbled
3	tablespoons olive oil
2	tablespoons white wine vinegar

1. Peel and slice onion into rings.
2. In a medium bowl stir together cold water and white vinegar.
3. Add onion slices and soak for 30 minutes. Rinse onions in fresh water and refrigerate until ready to assemble the salad.
4. Whisk olive oil and white wine vinegar, with a pinch of salt and pepper to make a quick vinaigrette
5. Slice tomatoes.
6. Place one onion round on plate, and top with tomato slices.
7. Dress lightly with vinaigrette, add blue cheese crumbles to taste, and season with salt and coarsely cracked black pepper.

Tomato Chile Soup

Serves 4-6
Shitty Wine Beaters: Spice, Salt

Notes: The combination of peppers was what was on hand, and that's what is in the recipe. But the makeup of the chile mixture can certainly be varied, and you should use whatever suits you, or whatever is easily available. Home grown or farmers' market tomatoes will always beat store bought. The chipotles are dried and smoked jalapeños. They aren't absolutely necessary, but give a nice warm flavor in dishes. If you use a blender, puree in batches and put a towel over the top because blending hot stuff makes it expand, and you'll have soup splatters coming out of the top onto you and the rest of the kitchen.

3	tablespoons olive oil	3	cups chicken broth
2	green Anaheim (or California) chiles	1	teaspoon dried parsley
		½	teaspoon cumin
3	jalapeños	½	teaspoon oregano
1	red bell pepper, chopped	½	teaspoon white pepper
1	yellow onion, chopped	¼	teaspoon cayenne pepper, or to taste
4	cloves garlic, chopped		
6	tomatoes, chopped		sprigs of cilantro
2	canned chipotles, chopped		salt, pepper

1. Prepare the Anaheim and jalapeño chiles, as described below. Do not try to peel jalapeño.
2. Heat the olive oil in a large sauce pan, and add the onion and bell pepper. Cook for 3-4 minutes and add the garlic and cook for 1 minute longer.
3. Add the roasted chiles, tomatoes, chipotle, broth, parsley, cumin, oregano, white pepper, and cayenne. Simmer for 20 minutes.
4. Either pour the soup into a blender or use a hand-held immersion blender to puree the soup.
5. Season the soup to your taste, put in serving bowls, and garnish with the fresh cilantro. Serve with warm tortillas.
6. This soup is also very good cold. When serving cold, you can add a blob of sour cream and swirl it in.

Preparing Chiles

If you have a gas range, place the chiles over the flame and turn with tongs until they get blistered all over. You can also use the broiler and a foil lined baking sheet, but be sure to turn the chiles frequently and rearrange them periodically so they blister at the same rate. After the chiles are blistered all over, put them in a bag (paper or zipper lock) and steam for 15 minutes or so. After removing from the bag, peel off the skins with your fingers. If you want to keep the chiles whole (for rellenos, for example), make a small slit near the top and pull out the pith with the seeds attached. Rinse the insides to get the rest of the seeds. If you are going to chop the chiles, cut off the top, then make a cut down the side of the chile, open it up, and scrape out the seeds and pith with a knife.

White Bean and Kale Soup

Serves 6-8

Shitty Wine Beaters: Acid, Salt

Notes: You hear a lot of cooking personalities making jokes about the liquid in canned beans as if it's some horrifying concoction. Actually, it's pure beany goodness. It's water with a little salt that they cook the beans in, and the starch thickens it a bit. Salt and water are always welcome in our soups, which is why we don't drain the beans. A small metal perforated ball used for making tea with loose leaves is an easy way to get herbs into and out of a soup or stew. Keep Parmesan cheese rinds in your freezer, they add an incredible nutty, salty, umami-something to soups. Seasoning with vinegar is increasingly common. The vinegar works in a similar way to salt, muting your ability to taste bitter or sour flavors, thus enhancing savory ones.

1	pound Italian turkey sausage links	3	cups chicken stock
		1	bunch kale
2	tablespoons olive oil	1	3 ounce Parmesan rind (optional, but recommended)
1	tablespoon tomato paste		
1	teaspoon cumin	2	bay leaves
3	stalks celery	1	sprig rosemary
2	carrots	2	springs thyme
1	onion, chopped fine		salt and pepper
2	garlic cloves, minced or pressed		balsamic vinegar, for serving
4	15 oz. cans white beans		

1. Add 1 tablespoon olive oil to dutch oven over medium high and swirl to coat.
2. Remove sausage from casings and add to pot, breaking up sausage and cooking until no pink remains, about 5-6 minutes. Remove sausage to paper towel lined plate and set aside.
3. Ensure there is 1 tablespoon of fat in the pot, if not add up to 1 tablespoon oil.
4. Lower heat to medium, add tomato paste to the pot and cook for 2 minutes. Add cumin and cook for additional minute until mixture is dark, but avoid burning fond that develops.
5. Add celery, onion, carrots and 1 teaspoon salt ½ teaspoon pepper and cook slowly covered, for about 6-7 minutes. Check frequently and stir to ensure that vegetables are cooking evenly and that fond does not burn. If fond gets too dark, add 1 tablespoon water, scrape up browned bits and continue.
6. Add garlic and cook for 30 seconds. Add chicken stock, canned beans and the bean liquid.
7. Put herbs into loose tea ball or cheesecloth and add to pot. Add Parmesan rind, if using.
8. Simmer for 30-40 minutes uncovered to enable some evaporation.
9. About 15 minutes before serving, trim leaves from kale and chop roughly. Add to pot and ensure leaves are submerged. Continue simmering until kale is tender, about 15 minutes.
10. Serve with balsamic vinegar, preferably a thicker, aged balsamic.

Tortilla Soup

Serves 4
Shitty Wine Beaters: Salt, Spice

Notes: This is our substitute for chicken noodle soup, it is not only delicious, but seems like it kills viruses and bacteria. As they say, "it's good for what ails you." The tortilla strips can either be made from flour tortillas or corn tortillas, and if you don't want to make them, use tortilla chips out of the bag. The garnishes really make it special, in particular a wedge of lime, chopped cilantro, avocado slices, and a hard white grated cheese, either Mexican cotija or Parmesan. Look for the cotija, it's worth it. Yes, you may use tortilla chips out of the bag in the soup; if they are very large you may want to crumble them. Even better, you can also fry your own from cut up fresh corn tortillas. Add more white pepper before serving, if desired. But taste it first -- this is the heat!

6	cups chicken broth	2	cups chopped tomatoes
5-6	chicken tenders or 2 breasts, cubed	3	cloves garlic, minced
1	teaspoon cumin	2	four ounce cans chopped green chiles
1	teaspoon chili powder	½	teaspoon white pepper
1	tablespoon vegetable oil	1	lime wedges
1	teaspoon butter		chopped cilantro
1	cup chopped onion		avocado slices
1	celery stalk, chopped		grated hard cheese, Mexican or Parmesan
1	large or 2 small carrots, chopped		
3	tablespoons flour		

1. Heat broth, cumin, and chili powder in a pot over medium heat, then add the cubed chicken. Reduce heat to medium low to keep warm, but do not boil.
2. Heat the oil and butter in a 12 inch skillet over medium high heat.
3. When the butter and oil are hot, add the chopped onion, celery, and carrot, and cook 3-4 minutes, stirring frequently.
4. Add the garlic, tomatoes, and green chiles. Cook for another 3-4 minutes, and add the flour. Stir to incorporate the flour and cook for another 1-2 minutes to ensure no raw flour taste remains.
5. Add about 1 cup broth from chicken pot to the skillet; broth will combine with flour a form a paste. Adjust thickness with more broth if needed to make a smooth paste. Then add all the vegetable/flour paste mixture to the pot with the chicken, and stir to combine.
6. Let soup simmer over medium or medium low heat for fifteen or twenty minutes, covered, to let the flavors meld.
7. Meanwhile, fry the tortilla strips, or open the tortilla chip bag.
8. Put soup into bowls, and garnish with avocado, cheese, cilantro, tortilla strips, etc.

Potatoes Lyonnaise

Serves 6
Shitty Wine Beaters: Fat, Salt

Notes: This is a variation on the excellent potatoes at Morton's steakhouse. The only real difference is that theirs comes with a side of $65 prime aged porterhouse. Carmelizing onions takes way longer than most cookbooks say, we're not sure why they all lie like they do. The good news is that carmelized onions freeze beautifully, so a giant bag of Costco onions and rainy day is all you need to get a good stash for your freezer. See below for the process. As with our Bacon Quiche, even if you like more tender bacon it's better to cook it until very crisp. Otherwise the bacon with end up too soft and limp.

3	russet potatoes
1/3	pound thick cut bacon
3/4	cup carmelized onions
3	tablespoons butter
	salt and pepper

1. Peel potatoes and cut into ½ cubes. Do not rinse potatoes.
2. Place potatoes and 3 tablespoons butter into covered microwave-safe dish.
3. Microwave potatoes, covered, until cooked through, about 12-14 minutes total stirring about every 5 minutes.
4. Dice bacon into ¼ pieces and transfer to 12 inch nonstick skillet. Cook bacon over medium high until very crisp. Remove with slotted spoon, leaving fat in the skillet.
5. When potatoes are cooked, reheat skillet and bacon fat over medium high heat and add potatoes (and melted butter) to skillet, spreading out evenly. Cook until browned on the first side, about 5 minutes. Stir occasionally.
6. Continue cooking until potatoes are browned on all sides, about 6-8 minutes longer.
7. Lower heat to medium low and add carmelized onions and bacon bits. Stir to combine and heat through. Season to taste with salt and pepper.
8. Potatoes can be transferred to oven-safe baking dish and kept in 275 degree oven for 30 minutes, check and stir periodically to ensure the potatoes don't stick or burn.

Carmelized Onions: A large Dutch oven will handle about 7-8 large onions, but fill it all the way up to maximize your yield. Sweet onions like Vidalia are not advisable here, they come off as too sweet. Slice onion pole to pole to help retain shape. Add 1 tablespoon oil to Dutch oven and heat over medium low heat. Pile onions into Dutch oven, add 2 teaspoons salt and cover. Let onions cook very slowly, stirring occasionally until the onions wilt down and become more manageable. Fond development is a good thing, but if it ever gets too dark and threatens to burn add a couple tablespoons of water to deglaze. Scrape pot, the water will evaporate. Keep a close eye on fond development, and deglaze with water as needed. Cook about 1 to 1 ½ hours. Do a final deglaze with water. Cool and freeze in large zipper lock freezer bag. You can slice off portions of frozen onions as needed and return remainder to freezer.

Mashed Potatoes

Serves 4-6

Shitty Wine Beaters: Fat, Fat

Notes: Russet potatoes work the best for this dish, Yukon Gold in a pinch, but not red potatoes. A manual masher and whisk are all you need to process. Adding butter first before the cream is an essential step; it coats the starch molecules in fat and prevents gummy potatoes. Here's a Thanksgiving tip – make these potatoes a couple hours before dinner and put into your crock pot on low. They don't even need to be stirred, the taste and texture is the same as if you had just made them. And it frees up valuable cook top space and the hassle of trying to reheat potatoes without scorching.

4-6	small Russet potatoes
6-8	tablespoons butter
½	cup heavy cream (or half and half, or milk)
	white pepper
	salt

1. Peel about one potato per person (1/2 potato if they are large), dropping them in a pot of water as you peel them to keep the air off. (The air makes them turn brown.)
2. After they are all peeled, take them out of the water one by one, chop them into even chunks, and put them back in the water.
3. Drain the potatoes, and add fresh water just to cover them, swirl the water and drain again.
4. Add fresh water to cover the potatoes by 1 inch.
5. Put over medium high heat and bring to a boil. Reduce heat if needed, but maintain boil.
6. Cook for 15-20 minutes until easily pierced with paring knife a long fork. When they are soft to the center, remove from heat and drain the potatoes.
7. Let them dry slightly, and add 1-2 tablespoons of butter per spud (or more to taste).
8. Cover the potatoes to let the butter melt.
9. Using potato masher mash butter into potatoes. Stir them as you mash them, to incorporate the butter throughout.
10. Add heavy cream or milk a few ounces at a time. Once mashed, switch to a whisk to continue stirring.
11. Add salt and white pepper for seasoning.
12. Taste and add more butter, cream or seasoning as desired.

Classic Potato Salad

Serves 6
Shitty Wine Beaters: Fat, Fat, Salt

Notes: Andrea Geary over at Cooks Illustrated deserves a Nobel Prize for figuring out a foolproof way to cook eggs. She focused on soft boiled, but her method also allows for fast and perfect hard boiled eggs that are not over cooked and dry. The eggs will have a very dark yolk that's fully cooked but maintains more moisture than typical hard boiled eggs. See below for technique. Do not rinse potatoes after step 1, starch is our friend here. Dice onion several hours in advance if possible to tame onion bite if your onions are particularly strong. Getting the potatoes boiled perfectly is the only tricky part; too firm and the potatoes will have some unpleasant crunch to them, too soft and they turn to mush when you stir the salad together. If in doubt, before they feel completely cooked, turn heat off and let potatoes continue to cook slowly until they reach the desired consistency. Lots of mayo is recommended, and while perhaps not a super healthy choice, the goal at hand is to thwart an obnoxious Chardonnay that should never have been bottled let alone sold.

4	large russet potatoes
4	hard boiled eggs (see below)
1	small onion, diced
4	stalks celery, cut into small dice
1	cup Best Foods mayonnaise, or as desired
	salt and pepper

1. Peel potatoes and cut into ½ pieces.
2. Place potatoes in large saucepan or Dutch oven and cover with water by 1 inch.
3. Bring potatoes to boil, then reduce to medium and cook potatoes until tender, about 20 minutes. Potatoes should be very easily pierced with a paring knife, but not falling apart into mush.
4. Drain potatoes, then spread out on rimmed baking sheet and cool for 10 minutes, then transfer baking sheet to refrigerator to cool completely, at least 60 minutes, preferably longer.
5. Chop hard boiled eggs into rough pieces.
6. In large bowl combine cooled potatoes, chopped eggs, celery and onion to taste. Add ½ cup mayonnaise, then add ¼ cup at a time until desired consistency is reached. As is often the case with fat, more is better.
7. Adjust seasoning with salt and pepper.

Perfect hard boiled eggs
Place steamer basket in small saucepan and add 1 inch of water. Cover and bring water to a boil. Add 1-6 eggs, straight from the refrigerator, and steam for 11 minutes. Run cool tap water over eggs for 30 seconds to stop cooking process. Leaving eggs in pan, remove steamer basket and add ice cubes to saucepan to cool eggs completely. Peel, and proceed with Step 5 above.

Pan Roasted New Potatoes

Serves 4-6

Shitty Wine Beaters: Salt

Notes: The beauty of this recipe is that it's basically foolproof. The water evaporates after cooking the potatoes, but the fat stays behind in the skillet to make sure the potatoes crisp up beautifully. If the water has evaporated before the potatoes are fully cooked, just add a bit more water and continue cooking. If there's still water in the skillet once the potatoes are done, just increase heat to evaporate it away. Select potatoes that are no more than 2 inches in diameter if possible. Potatoes need to fit in the bottom of the skillet in a single layer for browning. You can make this with olive oil only, but the butter assists with browning.

8-10	small red or white potatoes, halved
1	tablespoon butter
2	tablespoon olive oil
1	bay leaf
	salt

1. Place halved potatoes cut side down in single layer in 12 inch nonstick skillet.
2. Add water until it comes halfway up the sides of the potatoes.
3. Add butter and olive oil, bay leaf and one teaspoon salt to water.
4. Heat skillet over high heat until water comes to a boil, then reduce heat to medium and cover.
5. Cooking time will vary based on the size of potatoes, about 13-15 minutes. Check with paring knife for doneness after 10 minutes.
6. If water has evaporated and potatoes are not yet tender, add ¼ cup water and continue cooking. Repeat as necessary until potatoes are done.
7. Once the water has evaporated the butter and olive oil will start sizzling, and potatoes will brown. Adjust heat to keep potatoes sizzling without burning. Toss potatoes to crisp other side, cook for 3-4 minutes, season with salt and pepper, remove bay leaf and serve.

Grandma's Green Beans

Serves 4-6
Shitty Wine Beaters: Salt, Acid

Notes: Here's an alternative to the modern barely-cooked vegetables you are used to getting in restaurants. This is old fashioned comfort food, which will add a pleasing satisfaction to almost any meal. You will need a ham hock for this recipe. They are available in almost all markets, sometimes two or three to a package. If you're only doing enough beans for four or five people, you only need one hock, and you can freeze the others for later. You can also use a ham steak instead of the hock, with similar results. You want to use a sauce pan where beans and hock are about the same level in the pan, to ensure everything is covered, but the amount of water is minimized.

1	pound fresh green beans
1	smoked ham hock
	salt and pepper
	tabasco (optional)

1. Wash the beans and pick them over and discard any stems or wilted beans.
2. Today's varieties of beans don't have much in the way of a string, so take advantage of that by lining up six or seven beans in a row and whacking off the ends all at once. If the beans are very long, you might also cut them in half at this point.
3. Put the ham hock, beans, and enough water to cover everything. You don't need to add salt; the ham hock will take care of that. But sprinkle with pepper, bring to a boil, and simmer for at least two hours.
4. Near the end, take out the hock, which may be in more than one piece at this point, and let it cool so you can handle it.
5. When cool, chop it up so that you can separate the bits of ham from the rest, and add the ham bits back into the beans. Add some butter, and, if needed, some salt and pepper to finish.
6. You can serve them as is, or add a little Tabasco or cider vinegar.

German Red Cabbage

Serves 5-6
Shitty Wine Beaters: Acid, Salt

Notes: This is a great cabbage recipe, and is a classic accompaniment to German food. Look for a halved cabbage if available at the supermarket.

3	tablespoons oil, preferably bacon fat, if you want to be authentic
½	small or 1/2 large head of red cabbage, shredded (about 1 1/2 pounds)
2	large or 3 small apples, peeled and chopped, preferably tart green variety
1	cup water
¼	cup sugar
1	teaspoon salt
½	teaspoon pepper
¼	teaspoon ground cloves
¼	cup white vinegar

1. Heat the oil or fat over medium heat in a large saucepan, add the cabbage and apple.
2. Cook, stirring frequently, 4-5 minutes to wilt cabbage.
3. Add water, sugar, salt, pepper, and cloves and bring to a boil.
4. Simmer for 45 minutes, stirring occasionally.
5. Just prior to serving, stir in the vinegar.

Toasted Corn Skillet

Serves 2-4
Shitty Wine Beaters: Salt

Notes: This is a quick, easy and tasty side dish. And you can use it to clean out whatever extra veggies you have in the fridge, adjust the quantities of each according to your tastes. The key to this dish is to let the corn get really toasted and brown, it adds a deep and nutty flavor. This can be a bit unnerving the first time you make it, especially when it starts popping and jumping out of the pan. The vegetables are cut very small for this dish (smaller than a stir fry), which makes it quick for them to cook through and brown. You can easily make this for a crowd, just use a Dutch oven, or make it in batches and keep warm.

2-4	ears fresh corn
2	tablespoons olive oil
1	cup broccoli florets
1	cup cauliflower florets
½	onion, chopped fine
1	fresh mild chile, Anaheim or similar
½	red, yellow or orange bell pepper

1. Shuck corn and remove silk. Strip kernels from cob by standing ears on ends and running a knife down the length of the cob, rotating the cob until all kernels are removed.
2. Cut all other vegetables into a fine dice.
3. Heat 2 tablespoons olive oil in 12 inch nonstick skillet over high heat until smoking. Add all vegetables at once, stir to coat, then smooth into even layer and cook without stirring.
4. Keep an eye on the corn to make sure it doesn't burn, but it will get spotty brown and begin to pop.
5. Once thoroughly browned on the first side, stir vegetables and continue to cook, stirring frequently until vegetables are tender and browned.
6. Season with salt and pepper and serve.

Hoppin' John

Serves 2-4
Shitty Wine Beaters: Salt

Notes: Many people make it a policy to eat blackeye peas on New Year's Day for good luck. So where does a goofy name like Hoppin' John come from? Well, the most reasonable explanation is that in Creole Country, where the dish originated, blackeye peas are called "pigeon peas". In French, that is *pois pigeons,* which is pronounced "pwah peeJON". Good enough for us. This Hoppin' John is really good and is a great accompaniment to many dishes. And it's got the ingredients for good luck for the coming year: blackeye peas for pocket change and collard greens for folding money. This recipe uses fresh, canned or frozen (not dried) blackeye peas. The reason the ham hocks are better used in this recipe than the ham pieces is that the water the hocks boil in gets a great flavor that is missing otherwise.

3	cartons fresh blackeye peas, or two 15 ounce cans, or two packages frozen
2	ham hocks, cooked and shredded (or leftover ham)
1	large onion, chopped
1	green pepper, chopped
3	cups cooked white rice
3	cups thawed cooked collard greens
1	teaspoon salt
½	teaspoon black pepper
1	teaspoon cayenne pepper (or more)

1. Score the rind of the ham hocks with a knife, and then boil them for 1/2 hour or more in enough water to cover them.
2. Remove and drain the ham hocks, but reserve cooking water.
3. When hocks are cool enough to handle, tear them apart, discarding all but the pieces of ham. Shred or chop up the larger pieces of ham.
4. While ham hocks are boiling, prepare rice according to package directions.
5. Boil the blackeye peas in the same water that you cooked the ham hocks in, until they are tender to the bite. (Canned peas will cook faster.) Drain peas, return to pot, and set aside.
6. Sauté the onion and green pepper in 1 teaspoon oil in a skillet for a few minutes and add to the peas. Add the ham, collard greens, and rice, and heat to meld the flavors.
7. Serve it as a side dish, or over corn bread. It's also really good seasoned with Tabasco or with a spoonful of salsa on top.

Rooster Steak Sauce

Serves 2-4
Shitty Wine Beaters: Fat, Spice, Salt

Notes: No, this isn't a sauce for rooster steaks. This steak sauce gets its name from the chile-garlic sauce with a picture of a rooster on the bottle. It's from the same folks that bring us Sriracha, so you know it's good. This is an example of a pan sauce, in this case made in the skillet after cooking a steak.

1	tablespoon oil (either fat left over after cooking the steak, or added olive oil)
1	tablespoon flour
¼	cup red wine
1 ½	tablespoons Rooster sauce
2	teaspoons chopped thyme
1	teaspoon chopped tarragon
1	teaspoon lime juice
1	teaspoon A-1 sauce
¼	teaspoon Worcestershire sauce
4	tablespoons (1/2 stick) butter, cold, cut in pieces

1. Remove steaks from skillet, and add oil, if needed, to equal 1 tablespoon.
2. Heat (or re-heat) the oil, add the flour, and stir to make a roux. Cook, stirring constantly, for 3 minutes to ensure no flour taste remains.
3. Add red wine and deglaze the pan, scraping up any bits clinging to the pan. Add the remaining ingredients except for the butter and stir to combine. Simmer for 3-4 minutes.
4. Add the butter one piece at a time, whisking constantly to incorporate it into the sauce.
5. Keep warm until served.

Basic Tomato Sauce

Shitty Wine Beaters: Acid, Salt

Notes: This is a variation on Mario Batali's basic tomato sauce. He adds a grated carrot, which we discovered after making it 50 times that we never actually notice in the finished sauce. This is not a classic marinara, which we have found to sometimes be too thick, heavy and sweet. This is a lighter and fresher sauce, tasting more like actual tomatoes. Unlike fresh tomatoes which are picked green, canned whole tomatoes are picked after they ripen on the vine and are a much better option for sauces. This sauce is great for light pasta dishes, chicken Parmesan, or as a pizza sauce. The limited herbs and spices here are intentional, making the sauce more versatile. But you can add other herbs, such as basil, if desired. Double the recipe and freeze extra for future use.

¼ cup olive oil
1 large onion, chopped
2 teaspoons kosher salt
3 cloves garlic, pressed or minced
2 teaspoons dried oregano
2 28 ounce cans whole peeled tomatoes

1. Open canned tomatoes and using kitchen shears cut tomatoes into pieces.
2. Heat olive oil in large saucepan over medium heat until shimmering.
3. Add onion and salt and sauté until translucent, about 4-5 minutes.
4. Add garlic and oregano and sauté until fragrant, about 30 seconds.
5. Add tomatoes to saucepan and heat until simmering vigorously.
6. Reduce heat to medium low and simmer gently until tomatoes break down, about 20 minutes.
7. Remove saucepan from heat and, using immersion blender, blend using short pulses until there are no remaining tomato chunks and sauce is at desired consistency.
8. If sauce is thinner than desired, simmer until desired consistency is reached, 5-10 minutes longer.
9. Adjust seasoning (salt, oregano, pepper) as desired.
10. Once cooled, use immediately or batch freeze in two cup containers.

Stay up-to-date with us:

pairingwithshittywine.com

cookingdude.com

readerplace.com

11620747R00052

Made in the USA
Monee, IL
13 September 2019